Julia Child

A Little Golden Book® Biography

By Kari Allen

Illustrated by Joanie Stone

For Madon, my chef. And to Aunt Kathy and Aunt Roe,
your kitchens contain magic. —K.A.

 A GOLDEN BOOK • NEW YORK

Text copyright © 2024 by Kari Allen
Cover art and interior illustrations copyright © 2024 by Joanie Stone
All rights reserved. Published in the United States by Golden Books, an imprint of
Random House Children's Books, a division of Penguin Random House LLC, 1745 Broadway,
New York, NY 10019. Golden Books, A Golden Book, A Little Golden Book, the G colophon,
and the distinctive gold spine are registered trademarks of Penguin Random House LLC.
rhcbooks.com
Educators and librarians, for a variety of teaching tools, visit us at RHTeachersLibrarians.com
Library of Congress Control Number: 2023951576
ISBN 978-0-593-70334-2 (trade) — ISBN 978-0-593-70335-9 (ebook)
Printed in the United States of America
10 9 8 7 6 5 4 3 2 1

Julia Child was born Julia Carolyn McWilliams in Pasadena, California, on August 15, 1912. She lived with her mother, father, and younger brother and sister.

As a child, Julia had no interest in cooking. No one knew she would grow up to become one of the world's most famous chefs.

One of Julia's first food memories was eating a Caesar salad. When she was fourteen years old, her family took a trip to Tijuana, Mexico. They dined at Caesar Cardini's restaurant, and the famous chef himself came to the table to prepare the salad. Julia never forgot how he cracked the eggs for the special dressing.

Growing up, Julia was athletic, strong, and tall! At six feet two, she was captain of her high school basketball team. She also performed in plays and was student council president.

After high school, Julia attended Smith College, an all-women's school in Northampton, Massachusetts. There, she studied history and played more basketball. After she graduated in 1934, Julia wasn't sure what she wanted to do next. She tried to be a writer and a secretary, but neither of those things felt right.

When World War II broke out, Julia tried to enlist in the Women's Army Corps—but they told her she was too tall! Instead, she went to work for the Office of Strategic Services, which later became the Central Intelligence Agency, or CIA. Her job involved keeping track of top-secret information and helping make a shark repellent to protect pilots who landed in the sea.

In 1944, Julia was stationed in Ceylon (now known as Sri Lanka), a country in Asia. There she met her future husband, Paul Child. Paul was a photographer and an artist. He also loved a good meal!

On September 1, 1946, Julia and Paul got married in Lumberville, Pennsylvania. They lived in Washington, DC, for a short time before making the big move across the Atlantic Ocean to Paris, France.

Julia's first meal in France was at a restaurant called La Couronne. She had sole meunière—a fish in a brown butter sauce—and a long, thin bread called a baguette. She enjoyed every bite and fell in love with French food.

In 1949, Julia enrolled at Le Cordon Bleu, the famous French cooking school. The well-known chef Max Bugnard was her teacher.

Julia studied hard and perfected many difficult recipes. When it was time for the final exam, the students were tested on simple things like how to cook an oeuf mollet, a soft-boiled egg. Julia had prepared for more complex dishes and couldn't remember what an oeuf mollet was! She failed the exam and had to retake it to get her diploma.

But Julia was happy. She had finally found the thing she was meant to do.

In 1951, Julia met Simone Beck and Louisette Bertholle. The three new friends started a cooking school called L'École des Trois Gourmandes (The School of the Three Hearty Eaters). Simone and Louisette were also writing a cookbook about French cooking for Americans. They wanted an American to help them. Julia was the perfect choice.

Writing the cookbook wasn't easy. They had to make sure the recipes would work for an American cook. Grocery stores in America didn't always carry the same ingredients sold at a French market. And when Julia and Paul left Paris, much of the work had to be done through the post office. Since there were no personal computers back then, the women typed up their notes on typewriters and mailed them to each other.

It took nine years to write, revise, and perfect the cookbook. When *Mastering the Art of French Cooking, Volume I* was finally published in 1961, it was over seven hundred pages long and a huge success! At a time when most Americans were eating convenient, frozen, and fast meals, this book taught people how to slow down and enjoy the process of cooking.

To promote the new cookbook, Julia appeared on a
TV show in Boston called *I've Been Reading*. Instead of
simply talking about the book, Julia surprised everyone
by cooking an omelet right there on the set.

After it aired, the station received letters from people
who loved the show. They wanted to see more Julia!

The producers decided to give Julia her own show. On February 11, 1963, *The French Chef* debuted on public television. It aired first in Boston and then nationwide. Julia cooked fancy dishes like boeuf Bourguignon and French onion soup, explaining everything in her distinctive high-pitched voice.

The show was a hit! Viewers loved how Julia made complex recipes seem easy. They also loved that she sometimes made mistakes. Once, she accidentally flipped a potato pancake out of the pan, picked it up, and kept right on cooking! And they loved that she ended every show by saying "Bon appétit!" That means "Enjoy your meal!" in French.

The French Chef won a Daytime Emmy Award in 1966. It was the first time an educational television show ever won!

In 1973, after more than two hundred episodes, *The French Chef* ended. But Julia didn't rest for long. She went on to write more than fifteen cookbooks. She cooked on popular television shows like *Good Morning America* and *The Tonight Show*. She even cooked spaghetti with Mr. Rogers.

She created several more cooking shows, too. Julia was eighty-seven years old when she and her friend Chef Jacques Pépin starred in her last show, *Julia and Jacques Cooking at Home*. They made Julia's classic Caesar salad, inspired by the one she ate in Mexico as a girl.

Julia won many awards and honors throughout her career. In 1993, she was the first woman inducted into the Culinary Institute of America's Hall of Fame. She also received the Presidential Medal of Freedom from President George W. Bush in 2003.

In 2001, Julia donated her home kitchen to the Smithsonian Institution in Washington, DC. You can see her copper pots and pans, blue cabinets, and the counter that was built two inches taller than a standard counter so it would be high enough for Julia.

On August 13, 2004, Julia Child passed away at the age of ninety-one. She lived a full life, doing what she loved most: cooking and eating! She taught the world that with a bit of practice and patience anyone can make a delicious meal.

Bon appétit, Julia!